Sacagawea:

Guide for the Lewis and Clark Expedition

Hal Marcovitz

Chelsea House Publishers
Philadelphia

Prepared for Chelsea House Publishers by:
OTTN Publishing, Stockton, N.J.

CHELSEA HOUSE PUBLISHERS
Production Manager: Pamela Loos
Art Director: Sara Davis
Director of Photography: Judy L. Hasday
Managing Editor: James D. Gallagher
Senior Production Editor: J. Christopher Higgins
Series Designer: Keith Trego
Cover Design: Forman Group

3 5 7 9 8 6 4 2

Library of Congress Cataloging-in-Publication Data

Marcovitz, Hal.
    Sacagawea: guide for the Lewis and Clark Expedition
        / Hal Marcovitz.
        p.   cm. – (Explorers of new worlds)
Includes bibliographical references and index.
ISBN 0-7910-5959-6 (hc) – ISBN 0-7910-6169-8 (pbk.)
1. Sacagawea, 1786-1884–Juvenile literature. 2. Lewis
and Clark Expedition (1804-1806) –Juvenile literature.
3. Shoshoni women–Biography–Juvenile literature.
4. Shoshoni Indians–Biography–Juvenile literature.
[1. Sacagawea, 1786-1884. 2. Shoshoni Indians–Biography. 3. Indians of North America–Biography. 4.
Women–Biography. 5. Lewis and Clark Expedition
(1804-1806).] I. Title. II. Series.

F592.7.S123 M37 2000
978.0049745'0092–dc21
[B]   00-043595

Sacagawea:

Guide for the Lewis and Clark Expedition

Explorers of New Worlds

Contents

The gravestone reads:

SACAJAWEA
DIED APRIL 9 1884
A GUIDE WITH THE
LEWIS AND CLARK
EXPEDITION
1805 — 1806
IDENTIFIED 1907 BY
REV J ROBERTS
WHO OFFICIATED AT
HER BURIAL

An Outstanding Woman of History

This marker in the Wyoming prairie is believed to be the grave of Sacagawea, the Native American woman who helped Lewis and Clark explore the Northwest from 1804 to 1806.

I

n 1884, the Reverend John Roberts found himself living among the Shoshoni Indians on the Wind River Reservation in Wyoming. At the time, Wyoming was still an untamed frontier territory—a place of wild rivers and treacherous trails, snowcapped mountains where few people ventured, and forests so thick that a trapper could disappear into the trees and not see another human face for months.

The fur traders and cowboys who made their living in Wyoming's rugged countryside might see the *tepees* of Indians dotting the landscape of a reservation. The Crow, Cheyenne, and Arapaho Indians had settled in Wyoming. So had the Shoshonis.

Roberts was a *missionary*—a man sent by his church to convert the Indians to Christianity. He found the Shoshonis living peacefully on their reservation, having been uprooted from their lands after years of conflict with other Indians as well as with white settlers, who relentlessly pushed westward.

One day, Roberts was summoned to the tepee of an old woman. She was near death. It was said on the reservation that the woman had been born about 1790, which meant that she would be close to the age of 94. Roberts found friends and relatives gathered around the woman in her tepee. He asked her name. "Sacagawea," he was told.

The name of Sacagawea (sometimes spelled Sacajawea) was legendary among the Indians. From 1804 to 1806, a young Indian girl named Sacagawea had accompanied Meriwether Lewis and William Clark, the great American explorers, most of the way on their 8,000-mile journey from just outside St. Louis, Missouri, to the Pacific Ocean and back. Along with

BASIL,
SON OF
SACAJAWEA
DIED 1886
IN HIS
86TH
YEAR

Was the woman that missionary John Roberts (left) buried in 1884 actually Sacagawea, the Lewis and Clark guide?

her husband, a French Canadian fur trader named Toussaint Charbonneau, Sacagawea had helped Lewis and Clark open up a trail across the vast American West, serving as a guide and **interpreter**. Both Lewis and Clark gave a large measure of credit for the success of their **expedition** to the help provided by the Indian girl.

When Roberts was told the name of the woman who lay dying in front of him, he was shocked. Sacagawea was supposed to have died in 1812!

John Luttig, a fur trader, had kept a diary at Fort Manuel, an **outpost** in South Dakota. On December 20, 1812, he wrote: "This evening, the wife of Charbonneau, a [Shoshoni woman], died of a putrid fever. She was a good woman . . . aged about twenty-five years. She left a fine infant girl." Luttig wrote that Sacagawea was buried somewhere outside the gates of Fort Manuel. Her grave had never been found.

Historians would later find a notebook made by William Clark years after his famous expedition had ended. In the notebook, the old explorer had tried to account for the fates of the people who had accompanied him on the trek west. In his entry for Sacagawea, Clark had simply written: "Dead."

But perhaps Sacagawea had not died at Fort Manuel and was, in fact, the old woman that Roberts found in Wyoming in 1884. "Some of the old people told me that one of her granddaughters looks very much like the heroine did in former days," Roberts said years later. "She understood French well. The old lady had been wonderfully active and intelligent, considering her age. She walked alone and was bright to the last."

Another missionary, James I. Patten, also recalled meeting the old woman known as Sacagawea a few years before her death. He said that the woman spoke French and English, as well as several Indian languages. One day her two sons, Basil and Jean Baptiste, asked Patten to look after her while they went on a buffalo hunt. During his stay with the woman, she told him that she had accompanied Lewis and Clark in 1805, and that her son Jean Baptiste had been the little *papoose* whom she had carried on her back throughout the journey.

Inside the tepee, age finally overtook the old woman. She died on April 9, 1884. Her body was wrapped in animal skins, which were then sewn up for burial. She was placed across the back of a horse, which was then led to a Shoshoni cemetery on the Wind River Reservation. The body of the woman was placed in a wooden coffin and lowered into the grave. Today, that grave can still be found near Fort Washakie on the reservation. Her sons Jean Baptiste and Basil are said to be buried beside her.

Roberts officiated at her funeral. At first, a wooden marker was placed at the head of her grave. It was eventually replaced with a stone marker. Roberts later wrote: "I little realized that the heroine we laid to rest, in years to come, would become one of the outstanding women of American history."

The Corps of
Discovery

Sacagawea points the way for Meriwether Lewis and William Clark during their expedition. The two leaders considered her an invaluable member of the Corps of Discovery, as their party was called. Another important expedition member, Clark's slave York, is pictured at the far left.

2

Sacajawea was born in the Lemhi River Valley, near what is today known as Salmon, Idaho. It is a land of sagebrush, cottonwood trees, brown hills, and rugged mountains. The Shoshonis—sometimes known to their enemies as the Snakes—had settled in the Lemhi River Valley after years of war with neighboring tribes, such as the Blackfoot, Cree, Assiniboine, Crow, and Hidatsa.

Life was not easy for the Shoshonis. By the time

Sacajawea was born, the Shoshonis were surrounded by their enemies and forced to eke out a meager existence from the little wildlife they could trap in the valley. They built *weirs*—small earthen dams—in the streams to catch salmon. They picked berries and dug for roots and wild carrots. Many Indians starved. When the men of the tribe were lucky enough to kill a deer, they often fell on the animal's *carcass* and ate the flesh without cooking it.

Sometimes they ventured out of the valley in search of buffalo on the nearby plains. As a child, Sacajawea went along on many buffalo hunts. She grew familiar with the vast flatlands found beyond the mountains surrounding the Lemhi River Valley.

In the language of the Shoshonis, the name Sacajawea means "Boat Pusher." Perhaps at some time in her childhood, Sacajawea was given the job of pushing canoes along streams while the men leaned out of the boats to snag the salmon caught in the weirs.

One day, while camping on a prairie near what is now known as Three Forks, Montana—not too far from the Idaho border—the Shoshoni party was attacked by a band of Hidatsa Indians. Sacajawea and other young Shoshoni girls tried to escape across a shallow part of the Missouri River, but they were captured by Hidatsas.

It was not uncommon in those days for Indian tribes to kidnap each other's young and raise them as their own. That was what happened to Sacajawea. She was adopted by a Hidatsa family and raised as a member of their tribe.

During her years with the Hidatsas, she learned their language. The members of her new tribe also pronounced her name differently: "Sacagawea" instead of "Sacajawea." In Hidatsa, this name means "Bird Woman."

While Sacagawea was learning the ways of the Hidatsa, thousands of miles away in Washington, D.C., President Thomas Jefferson was taking steps that would forever change the face of the young nation known as the United States

Throughout history, Sacagawea's name has been spelled many different ways. Lewis and Clark themselves used 14 different spellings for the name of their guide. However, the English translation of the name Lewis and Clark used most frequently was "Bird Woman." This name spelled in the Hidatsa language translated most accurately to "Sacagawea"–with a hard "g" sound in the third syllable–rather than "Sacajawea," her Shoshoni name.

of America. In 1803, Jefferson completed the Louisiana Purchase, buying from France a huge tract of land that doubled the territory owned by the United States. The new territory, which consisted of more than 800,000 square miles, included what would become the states of North Dakota, South Dakota, Nebraska, Oklahoma, Arkansas, and Missouri, as well as parts of Louisiana, Minnesota, Kansas, Montana, Wyoming, and Colorado.

Much of the territory included in the Louisiana Purchase was wild and unexplored. Also, it was known that there was land farther west—a region containing vast forests, wide rivers, and rolling hills that stretched all the way to the Pacific Ocean. So Jefferson summoned his personal secretary, Meriwether Lewis, and assigned him the task of putting together an expedition to explore the new territory.

The job of the group that became known as the *Corps of Discovery* would be to find a trail from St. Louis to the Pacific Ocean. At the time, St. Louis was just a tiny village on the banks of the Mississippi River. Still, it was the last outpost of civilization on America's western frontier. The Missouri River, which flowed directly into the heart of the land included in the Louisiana Purchase, was located a

Thomas Jefferson, the third president of the United States, wanted to expand the country's boundaries. After purchasing a huge tract of land from France for $15 million, he sent Lewis and Clark to explore this enormous wild region.

few miles north of St. Louis. That river would take the explorers on the first leg of their journey.

Jefferson told Captain Lewis: "The object of your mission is to explore the Missouri River, and such principal streams of it, as by its course and communication with the waters of the Pacific Ocean, and to find out what may offer the most direct and practicable water communication across the continent, for the purpose of commerce."

In other words, Jefferson had envisioned the day when wagon trains and riverboats would make their way west carrying food and supplies for towns that would rise up out of the American frontier. Of

Twenty-nine-year-old Meriwether Lewis was Jefferson's choice to lead the expedition. Lewis had served as Jefferson's personal secretary. The president wanted Lewis to bring back a detailed record of everything he saw.

course, in 1803, he had no way of knowing that not only would wagon trains and riverboats one day follow the Lewis and Clark trail, but so would railroads and highways.

The members of the Corps of Discovery would be expected to draw maps, make peace with the Indians they found along the way, and take notes about the wildlife, plant life, and minerals the explorers would undoubtedly discover. It would be an incredibly long, difficult, and dangerous journey.

Lewis decided that he could not lead such an expedition alone. He called on Captain William Clark, a friend from his days in the army, to share

William Clark had served with Lewis in the army after the Revolutionary War. When Lewis was named leader of the Corps of Discovery, he asked the 33-year-old Clark to join the expedition and share in the leadership duties.

leadership of the Corps of Discovery.

Lewis and Clark spent the summer and fall of 1803 preparing for the journey and enlisting other members of the Corps of Discovery. They convinced 42 hunters, trappers, boatmen, and soldiers to make the trip. The Corps of Discovery remained in St. Louis for the winter of 1803—in those days, travelers did well to stay put during the harsh winter months. Finally, on May 14, 1804, members of the expedition headed up the Missouri River.

The first few months of the expedition unfolded slowly and without much excitement for the travelers, although it was during this time that the Corps of Discovery suffered its first, and only, death. On August 20, 1804, Sergeant Thomas Floyd died while the expedition traveled near what is now Sioux City, Iowa. Clark, who served as the medical officer for the trip, determined that the man had suffered a ruptured appendix—an ailment for which there was no cure in those days of primitive medicine and surgery. Incredibly, over the next three years, the Corps of Discovery would face harsh weather, treacherous mountains and rivers, hostile Indians, fierce grizzly bears and other wild animals, accidents, illnesses, and hunger—and every member of the corps would make it home safely.

On October 27, 1804, the Corps of Discovery reached the Five Villages of the Mandan Indians near present-day Bismarck, North Dakota. Lewis and Clark knew their first winter on the frontier was approaching. Clearly, it was time to make camp and rest until spring.

A few days later, they were approached by a French Canadian trapper named Toussaint Charbonneau, who offered his services to the Corps of Discovery as a cook and interpreter. Charbonneau told Lewis and Clark he could speak the Hidatsa language. The captains knew they would be encountering many Indian tribes as the expedition pushed westward, and at this point, nobody in the corps could communicate with the Indians. Charbonneau was soon given the job.

Charbonneau had a wife—a young Indian woman no more than 14 or 15 years old. Her name was Sacagawea. He had won her in a gambling game with the Hidatsa Indians and married her. She would make the trip as well. But Sacagawea was pregnant. On February 11, 1805, the Indian girl gave birth to a little boy. Charbonneau named his son Jean Baptiste. He would be carried on his mother's back as the Corps of Discovery made its way to the Pacific Ocean.

Finally, the weather improved. It was April 7, 1805. The day had arrived to continue the journey west. In his diary, Lewis wrote: "We are about to penetrate a country at least two-thousand miles in width on which the foot of civilized man has never trodden."

William Clark, who would grow very fond of Sacagawea's child, gave the baby the nickname "Pomp." It is said that Clark hoisted the child high above his head and playfully remarked that the baby reminded him of the ancient Roman general Pompey.

The Three Forks

In addition to her duties as a guide, Sacagawea was valuable to the Corps of Discovery as an interpreter, as shown in this river meeting. Her presence was also helpful in reassuring the Native Americans that the Corps of Discovery was on a peaceful mission of exploration— no war party would have women and children along.

3

It did not take long for trouble to find the Corps of Discovery—or for Sacagawea to prove her value to the expedition.

By mid-May 1805, the Corps of Discovery had made its way up the Missouri River and had crossed over into Montana. Some of the explorers traveled in a **keelboat**, a 50-foot-long wooden boat equipped with masts and sails, which also carried long poles so that the vessel could be pushed through shallow waters on calm days. Some of the men traveled in **pirogues**, small canoes fashioned from hollowed-out logs. And some of the explorers walked along the banks of the river, following close behind the boats.

On May 14, with Charbonneau at the helm of a pirogue, a sudden gust of wind struck the boat, nearly capsizing it. Panic struck the men on board. Some of them fell overboard, while others clung to the sides of the craft. Charbonneau, who was certainly no boatman, also panicked, dropping the boat's *tiller*. The pirogue quickly started filling with water.

Lewis and Clark were hiking along the shoreline, hundreds of feet away. Both captains dashed into the shallow river and tried to make their way to the pirogue, but they had to wade through the water and the going was slow. Finally, enough men reached the boat to steady the craft and set it back on its keel.

Sacagawea had been on the pirogue as well. When the boat turned over, she calmly waded out into the river and recovered much of the cargo that had been on board: food, clothing, hunting and trapping equipment, pathfinding tools, and gifts for the Indians.

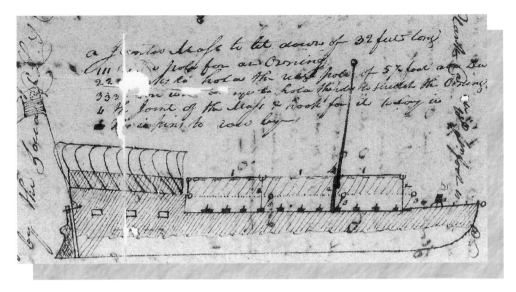

This drawing from Meriwether Lewis's diary shows the 50-foot-long keelboat that the explorers used on their trip up the Missouri River. The Corps of Discovery also used smaller craft, called pirogues.

Lewis noticed how Sacagawea had kept her head during the near-catastrophe and had made herself useful. He wrote in his diary: "The Indian woman, to whom I ascribe equal fortitude and resolution with any person on board at the time of the accident, caught and preserved most of the light articles which were washed overboard."

Two weeks later, the Corps of Discovery took a southwest fork of the Missouri River. After the expedition decided to make camp, Sacagawea became ill. "I found the Indian woman extremely ill," Clark wrote in his journal on June 13. "This gave me some concern, as well as for the poor object herself, then with a young child in her arms, as from her condition of being our only dependence for a friendly negotiation with the Snake Indians, on whom we depend for horses to assist us in our travel from the Missouri River to the Columbia River."

Clark, the expedition's medical officer, knew some home remedies and frontier-style cures and could treat the sick as well as any physician in those days. He found some water in a sulfur spring and ordered Sacagawea to drink. Apparently, the mineral water helped reduce Sacagawea's fever. "Now," Clark soon wrote, "her pulse has become regular, much fuller, and a gentle perspiration [has] taken place; the nervous system has also in great measure abated, and she feels herself much freer of pain."

Sacagawea's illness was one of many problems that had plagued the expedition. Lewis, Clark, and other men in the corps also had to endure fevers and injuries. The men were constantly attacked by swarms of mosquitoes and blackflies, which stung them and invaded their eyes, ears, and noses. Needle grass, a plant with barbed leaves, cut through the men's shoes. "They penetrate our moccasins and leather leggings and give us great pain until they are removed," wrote Clark.

Food was often scarce. The men preferred to eat deer and small game that they could shoot with their rifles. But game was often hard to find, and many times the hunters returned to camp empty-handed. Sacagawea taught them how to *forage* for food in the woods, demonstrating where to find berries and edible roots. One day, the men were lucky enough to bag an elk. Days later, when the meat was gone, Sacagawea showed them how to stretch a few more suppers out of their catch by breaking the bones open and scraping the *marrow*—a soft, edible tissue—from their insides.

"She broke two shank bones of the elk after the marrow was taken out, boiled them and extracted a pint of grease or tallow from them," wrote Lewis.

To a hungry man out on the trail, berries, roots, and the scrapings from hollow bones must have been as delicious as any hunk of deer meat.

Sacagawea soon recovered from her fever, and the Corps of Discovery pushed on. The expedition arrived at a series of steep waterfalls which they would have to *portage* around. This meant the men had to leave the river, hoist the boats onto primitive carts, and make their way over a series of trails to a point below the falls where they could reenter the river. This detour would take them along 18 rugged, difficult miles. To make matters worse, a sudden storm blew up. Clark, Charbonneau, Sacagawea, and Pomp were nearly swept away by a flood caused by a **cloudburst**. But they took shelter beneath an overhanging rock and waited out the storm.

By mid-July, the Corps of Discovery had made its way to an area near what is now Helena, Montana. Sacagawea told Lewis and Clark that she was familiar with the region: she remembered it from her days as a young girl growing up among the

This is the remains of one of the peace medals carried by Lewis and Clark to present to Indian leaders they met along the way. The other side of the medal was engraved with the image of Thomas Jefferson.

Shoshoni tribe. On July 25, the explorers reached Three Forks, a point where the Missouri branched off into three **tributaries**. Lewis and Clark named the waterways the Jefferson, Madison, and Gallatin Rivers in honor of the president as well as two cabinet officers: James Madison, the secretary of state, and Albert Gallatin, the secretary of the treasury. Lewis and Clark decided to follow the Jefferson River, and three days later the explorers set up camp on Shoshoni land. Not too far from the camp, Sacagawea recognized some hills and told the captains that her people could be found just a few miles west down the Jefferson River.

Captain Lewis wondered what Sacagawea could be thinking. She had now returned to the land she had known as a child.

"She does not show any distress at these recollections or any joy at the prospect of being restored to her country," Lewis wrote in his diary. "She seems to possess the folly or the philosophy of not suffering her feelings to extend beyond the anxiety of having plenty to eat and a few trinkets to wear. I believe she would be perfectly content anywhere."

Explorers of New Worlds

Reunion
with the
Shoshonis

The members of the Lewis and Clark expedition meet Shoshoni Indians in the Lemhi River Valley. The encounter was a joyful one for Sacagawea, because she was reunited with her brother, now a chief of the tribe.

4

he Corps of Discovery broke camp and made its way west. Soon, the Jefferson River divided into three more forks. This time, the men took the central fork, which they named the Beaverhead River. On August 11, Captain Lewis took a small party to explore some trails. Within a few days they met a Shoshoni Indian on horseback. They offered him gifts, but it was clear the man did not understand their intentions. Suddenly, he commanded his horse to gallop away and disappeared into the countryside.

Two days later Lewis encountered three Shoshoni women. Again, the white men offered gifts and tried to communicate that their mission was peaceful. This time the gifts were accepted. Lewis managed to convince the Shoshonis to lead the explorers to their village.

Meanwhile, the rest of the Corps of Discovery had traveled along the Beaverhead River. Soon they saw a group of Shoshonis on horseback.

In his diary, Captain Clark wrote: "I saw at a distance several Indians on horseback coming towards me. Charbonneau and Sacagawea who were before me at some distance danced for the joyful sight, and she made signs to me that they were her nation. As I approached nearer them, I discovered one of Captain Lewis's party with them dressed in their dress. They met me with great signs of joy."

The Corps of Discovery was reunited on August 17 in the Lemhi River Valley in Idaho, not far from Sacagawea's place of birth. Sacagawea was in tears as she met many old friends whom she hadn't seen since she was a young child. But for Lewis and Clark, there was important business to conduct.

They were anxious to meet the Shoshoni chief, Cameahwait, and to make peace with him. They also needed horses for the journey across the mountains, which they hoped Cameahwait could provide. They intended to ask Cameahwait for guides to lead the journey farther west.

They sat down with Cameahwait in his tepee. Other ranking members of the tribe joined the **council**. But first, they would need Sacagawea to interpret. She was summoned to the chief's tepee.

When Sacagawea arrived, her face immediately broke into a broad smile because she recognized Cameahwait as her brother. There was a happy reunion as brother and sister rushed to each other.

"She jumped up, ran and embraced him and threw her blanket over him and cried profusely," wrote Captain Clark.

The council began. To communicate with Cameahwait, Lewis and Clark had to first give their message in English to Private Francis Labiche, who spoke French.

> **The joyful reunion of Cameahwait and Sacagawea didn't last long. Sadly, the chief told his sister the fates of other members of their family. All had died, except another brother and a nephew.**

The Shoshonis helped guide Lewis and Clark through the Bitterroot Mountains.

Labiche would then provide the message in French to Charbonneau. Charbonneau translated the words into Hidatsa, which Sacagawea understood. Finally, Sacagawea translated the words into Shoshoni for Cameahwait.

Despite the tedious route the words had to take back and forth, the message got through. Cameahwait agreed to provide 29 horses to the Corps of Discovery. Four Shoshoni guides would also accompany the expedition, at least part of the way. In return, Lewis and Clark gave the Shoshonis some tobacco, clothing, and deer meat.

The expedition left the Shoshoni village on August 29. Soon the men began the treacherous crossing of the Bitterroot Mountains. Progress was slow. Although it was late summer, nights in the mountains were cold. On September 4, the corps suffered a near-catastrophe when several men and horses fell down a steep slope. The men emerged from the accident with only minor wounds and injuries, but several of the horses died. Three of the Shoshoni guides turned back.

Finally, on September 20, the members of the Corps of Discovery emerged from the Bitterroot Mountains and found themselves looking over a vast plain. Within days, they encountered members of the Nez Percé tribe. They were taken to the Nez Percé village, where they made peace with the chief, Twisted Hair. After spending several days with the Nez Percé, Lewis and Clark decided to continue the journey by canoe along the Clearwater River, which would soon become the Columbia River—the vast waterway that serves as the border between the states of Washington and Oregon. On October 9, after bidding farewell to the fourth Shoshoni guide, the Corps of Discovery set out on what would be the final leg of the journey to the Pacific Ocean.

A Pilot through the Country

A group of Indians notice the Lewis and Clark expedition on the river in this painting by Charles M. Russell. William Clark would later write that Sacagawea had been "of great service . . . as a pilot through this country."

5

"Great joy in camp!" wrote Captain Clark on November 8. "We are in view of the ocean, this great Pacific Ocean which we have been so long anxious to see, and the roaring or noise made by the waves breaking on the rocky shores may be heard distinctly."

It was true. After traveling 4,100 miles on a journey that had started in St. Louis some 19 months before, the Corps of Discovery had finally made it to the Pacific

Ocean. President Jefferson's orders had been carried out. Lewis and Clark had crossed the lands of the Louisiana Purchase and found a route to the west coast.

Of course, the journey was not over. Winter was approaching, so the Corps of Discovery would have to find a place to make camp until the following spring. Then they would face the long and dangerous journey back east.

On December 7, the Corps of Discovery made camp near what is today Astoria, Oregon, on a south bend of the Columbia River very near the Pacific. They built eight cabins surrounded by a *stockade* and named the camp Fort Clatsop, after the Clatsop Indians who lived in a nearby village.

It would not be a pleasant winter. True, the climate at Fort Clatsop was more agreeable than what the explorers had encountered elsewhere. It was certainly far less cold on the Oregon coast than in the mountains of Montana. But the winter was constantly damp and Fort Clatsop was often shrouded in a dense fog. Many of the explorers fell ill with fever. Food was also scarce. "Oh, how disagreeable is our situation during this dreadful winter," Captain Clark wrote in his diary.

A sketch of Fort Clatsop, where Sacagawea spent the winter of 1805–6 with the Corps of Discovery.

Still, there was work to do. Lewis spent his days at Fort Clatsop making notes on the trees, shrubs, ferns, fish, reptiles, and birds he found near the camp. Clark worked on maps of the region. The men fixed their clothes and fashioned new moccasins. They became friendly with the Clatsop Indians and traded with them. One day an Indian told the explorers that a dead whale had washed up on a nearby beach.

What a sight to see! What better way to break the doldrums of the long winter months!

Sacagawea begged to go along. Clark wrote in his diary: "She observed that she had traveled a long way with us to see the great waters, and now that a monstrous fish was also to be seen, she thought it very hard not to be permitted to see that."

Clark, Charbonneau, Sacagawea, and other members of the corps ventured out of the stockade in search of the whale. Charbonneau had hoped to skin whale blubber from the animal and cook it for the hungry men. But the Indians had beaten them to the carcass. All the explorers found was a skeleton.

Still, they did not come home empty-handed. They traded with the Indians and obtained 300 pounds of blubber. Charbonneau prepared a fine feast for the explorers. Lewis wrote: "We thank the hand of providence for directing the whale to us, and think Him much more kind to us than

In general, the Corps of Discovery did not care for the Native Americans they met while at Fort Clatsop. Sergeant Gass, a member of the party, wrote: "All the Indians from the Rocky Mountains to the falls of Columbia, are an honest, ingenious and well disposed people; but from the falls to the seacoast, and along it, they are a rascally, thieving set."

He was to Jonah, having sent this monster to be swallowed by us instead of swallowing us."

Finally, the winter ended. On March 16, 1806, the Corps of Discovery broke camp and started the long journey home. The trip east would be no easier than the road west. In May, Pomp grew ill with fever and a swollen throat. He was now 15 months old. Clark treated the boy with a salve of beeswax and animal oil, and he recovered.

By June the Corps of Discovery once again found itself crossing the treacherous Bitterroot Mountains. Although summer would begin in a matter of days, the explorers had to lead their horses through deep snowdrifts. One man was injured after being thrown from his horse while crossing a creek. Two horses died in falls. Again, food was scarce. Conditions were so bad that the Corps of Discovery had to turn back. The explorers found their way out of the mountains and camped on a prairie not far from a Nez Percé village.

Lewis and Clark met with the Nez Percé chief and convinced him to supply the Corps of Discovery with some guides. After resting up, the expedition headed back into the Bitterroot Mountains. When they had originally arrived at the Bitterroots, they had hoped to make the crossing in five days. But now, 18 days had elapsed, and they still hadn't found a pass through the mountains.

But the Nez Percé guides knew the way. "They traverse this trackless region with instinct," wrote Lewis in his diary. "They are never embarrassed; and so undeviating is their step that whenever the snow had disappeared for even a hundred paces, we find the summer road." On June 29, led by their two Nez Percé guides, the Corps of Discovery emerged from the Bitterroot Mountains.

Lewis and Clark decided to split up. Lewis would take a northern route, crossing Idaho and Montana mostly by following the Missouri River. Clark would take a southern route, following first the Jefferson River and then the Yellowstone River east. They planned to meet at the mouth of the Yellowstone River just inside the North Dakota border. Charbonneau and Sacagawea accompanied Clark.

Clark's party soon found itself following Sacagawea. She knew the land and guided the explorers. She selected a route that took the travelers through the Bozeman Pass, an overland route in Montana that led the expedition from the banks of the Jefferson River to the Yellowstone River. "The Indian woman has been of great service to me as a pilot through this country," wrote Captain Clark.

The explorers also found the Bozeman Pass to be particularly easy to travel. During their trip through the pass, they were able to cross 48 miles in two days.

The Bozeman Pass was such a good route through Montana that, years later, the Northern Pacific Railroad would select Sacagawea's path as its route across that section of the territory.

Sacagawea was also providing a lot of food for the journey. The hunters weren't always able to bag game, so Sacagawea's skill at foraging for edible berries and roots was again crucial. Clark wrote that Sacagawea had provided the men with a "large, well-flavored gooseberry, of a rich crimson color, and a deep purple berry of a species of currant common on the river as low as the Mandans, and called . . . Indian currant."

Meanwhile, Captain Lewis and his men were encountering a rougher trail. In late July, Lewis's party met 30 Blackfeet Indians on horseback on the south fork of the Marias River, just west of where they planned to pick up the Missouri River. Lewis talked to them using sign language and gave them a

*Thirty years after the Lewis and Clark expedition, an
American artist named George Catlin followed their
route and painted many of the places that the explorers
had visited. This is a view of the Mandan village where
Sacagawea joined the Corps of Discovery, and where she
and her husband and son separated from them in 1806.*

flag, a medal, and a handkerchief as gifts. Uneasily,
Lewis's men and the Blackfeet made camp together.
But during the night, one of Lewis's men caught a
Blackfeet trying to steal his gun. In the ensuing fight,

two Indians were killed, one of them after being shot by Lewis. The other Indians rode off, but Lewis and his men feared they would return and attack the camp, so the explorers quickly packed up and headed for the trail. They rode hard, covering more than a hundred miles during the next two days.

On August 12, Lewis and Clark met up again on the Yellowstone River. Five days later, the weary travelers arrived back at the Five Villages of the Mandan Indians. The Corps of Discovery still had many miles to go before it reached St. Louis, but the Five Villages is where Charbonneau and Sacagawea had joined the expedition, and it turned out to be the place where they would leave the expedition.

For Sacagawea, the journey was over.

William Clark, shown here in a painting made years after the return of the Corps of Discovery, offered to help Sacagawea's son get an education as thanks for her help.

She Deserved a Greater Reward

6

*L*ewis and Clark invited Charbonneau and Sacagawea to stay with the expedition all the way to St. Louis, but Charbonneau declined. He was a fur trader, and the opportunities for him would be limited so close to civilization. In payment for his services as cook and interpreter, Charbonneau received a horse, two canoes, and a tent. Sacagawea received nothing. Captain Lewis wrote, "She deserved a greater reward for her attention and services on that route than we had in our power to give her."

Still, Captain Clark had grown particularly fond of Sacagawea and her son Pomp, and he offered to take

Pomp with him to St. Louis and raise the boy as his own son—paying for his education and introducing him to the customs of the civilized world. Charbonneau and Sacagawea declined the offer but said they would send the boy to Clark when he grew older.

The expedition departed the Five Villages, and Lewis and Clark soon found their way back to St. Louis. They completed this last leg of the journey in good time, sometimes covering as much as 50 miles in a single day.

On September 23, 1806, Clark wrote in his diary: "Descended to the Mississippi, and down that river to St. Louis at which place we arrived at 12 o'clock." The final act undertaken by the Corps of Discovery was to assemble in St. Louis and fire their rifles to announce their return and salute the town.

President Jefferson, who was delighted with the success of the expedition, rewarded Lewis and Clark each with 1,600 acres of land and about $1,200 in cash. (This was a great amount of money in those days.) The other members of the Corps of Discovery each received about 320 acres and $166.

Lewis went on to become governor of the Louisiana Territory, but he did not live long after the completion of the journey. Lewis became depressed

Sadly, Meriwether Lewis killed himself in 1809, just three years after the Corps of Discovery returned.

and started drinking heavily. He died in 1809 from a gunshot wound. It is believed he took his own life.

Clark became a general in the militia of the Louisiana Territory, and later became governor of the Missouri Territory and superintendent of Indian Affairs in St. Louis. Before he died in 1838, William

Clark kept his promise to Sacagawea. Her son Jean Baptiste Charbonneau, whom she had carried for most of the 8,000-mile journey, went to live with Clark, who raised the boy and sent him to school. Jean Baptiste learned to speak four languages and would later spend several years in Europe as the traveling companion of a German prince before returning to the American frontier. He traveled across the West, and it is believed he accompanied the famous American scout Kit Carson on many adventures.

In 1846, Jean Baptiste settled in California and served as the alcalde, or mayor, of the town of San Luis Rey. Later, Jean Baptiste Charbonneau caught gold fever, traveling to Idaho and Montana to prospect for gold and make his fortune. But he was said to have fallen ill and died in 1866, although other sources reported that he lived on the Shoshoni reservation with his mother and half-brother Basil into the 1880s.

After leaving the Corps of Discovery, Toussaint Charbonneau would live well into his 80s. At first he worked as a trapper, but in 1810 he tried farming a piece of land near St. Louis that he'd bought from William Clark. But Charbonneau soon realized he had no talent for tilling the soil. In 1811, he gave up the farm to join an expedition back up the Missouri River. This trip was headed by a trapper and explorer named Henry Breckenridge.

Breckenridge also kept a diary. In it he wrote, "We have on board a Frenchman named Charbonneau with his wife, an Indian woman of the Snake nation, both of whom accompanied Lewis and Clark to the Pacific, and were of great service. But she had become sickly and longed to revisit her native country; her husband also, who had spent many years among the Indians, was also becoming weary of a civilized life."

From there, the story of Sacagawea goes in two directions. One version reports that Sacagawea and Charbonneau stayed with the Breckenridge expedition until it arrived at Fort Manuel in South Dakota, where Sacagawea became ill and died in 1812, leaving behind an infant girl named Lizette. Another version reports that Charbonneau had taken two more Indian girls as wives—a custom not unusual for the times. Enraged, Sacagawea left Charbonneau and traveled from tribe to tribe until finally settling with the Shoshonis in Wyoming, where she lived out the last years of her life.

A statue of Sacagawea holding her infant son.
Many memorials have been erected to
commemorate Sacagawea's contribution to the
success of the Lewis and Clark expedition.

Repaying a National Debt

7

acagawea's contribution to the Corps of Discovery was recognized by Lewis and Clark when they named a stream in Montana Sacagawea Creek. In his diary, Lewis wrote: "A handsome river of about fifty yards in width discharged itself into the Mussellshell River. This stream we called Sah-ca-gah-we-ah or Bird Woman's River, after our interpreter the Snake woman."

The honors certainly didn't stop there. As Sacagawea's story was told and retold over the years, the governors and legislators in states where the young Indian woman had lived and explored all bestowed similar honors. Today you can find mountains named for Sacagawea in Montana, Wyoming, Oregon, and Idaho. There is a Lake Sacajawea in Washington and a Lake Skakakawea in North Dakota. Sacajawea State Park is located in Franklin County, Washington.

The Lewis and Clark trail itself is marked with many memorials to and reminders of the Indian guide. Visitors can find **plaques** and tablets commemorating Sacagawea in such places as Tendoy, Idaho; Armstead and Three Forks, Montana; and Mobridge, South Dakota. The grave marker of the woman thought to be Sacagawea who died in Wyoming is still in place.

Statues of Sacagawea stand in the state capitol in Bismarck, North Dakota; the Louisiana Purchase Exposition Grounds in St. Louis, Missouri; and the National Cowboy Hall of Fame in Oklahoma City, Oklahoma. Children attend public schools named for Sacagawea in Richland and Vancouver, Washington; Great Falls and Bozeman, Montana; and Lewiston, Idaho. Girl Scouts in Wyoming attend Camp Sacajawea. An airplane known as the *Spirit of Sacajawea* flew during the 1920s. And for many years, the U.S. Navy battleship *Wyoming* carried a silver table serving set that had the image of the brave Native American guide etched into the faces of the cups and plates.

"I have heard it said that Sacagawea is an obscure figure in American history," said Philip N. Diehl, director of the United States Mint. "Perhaps she is unknown to our generation, but she has not been obscure for most of our nation's history."

Diehl's remarks were made when the U.S. Mint announced that it had selected Sacagawea to replace Susan B. Anthony on the dollar coin. For years, the mint had been searching for a woman who had made contributions to American history for the new coin. Mint officials considered former first lady Eleanor Roosevelt, civil rights leader Rosa Parks, and Betsy Ross, the seamstress who is credited with sewing the first American flag, to replace Anthony, who led the fight to win the right to vote for American women. Finally, the mint selected Sacagawea.

"She was a member of no political party. She subscribed to no political ideology. She was simply a woman of exemplary physical courage and stamina, who through a remarkable confluence of circumstances contributed to the success of one of the greatest American adventures," Diehl said.

The front and back of the gold dollar coin that features Sacagawea's image. The coin was first issued in 2000.

The Anthony dollar had generally been considered a failure by mint officials. It was smaller than previous silver dollars, so it was often mistaken for a quarter. The mint produced 847.5 million Susan B. Anthony dollars in 1979 and 1980, but stopped their production when it became clear that people were simply refusing to use the coins.

The Sacagawea dollar is the same size as the Anthony dollar, but there are many differences that set it apart. For example, it is gold-colored. The Sacagawea dollar is round (the Anthony dollar actually had 11 sides) and has raised borders. The "heads" side depicts Sacagawea carrying her infant son on her back; the "tails" side includes an image of a bald eagle. The image of Sacagawea on the coin was conceived by Glenna Goodacre, an artist who designed the Vietnam Women's Memorial in Washington, D.C., and Thomas Rogers, an engraver at the U.S. Mint in Philadelphia.

"The story of Sacagawea is rich with the symbols and values that make our nation great," said the U.S. Mint's Philip Diehl. "It is fitting and proper that after almost two hundred years, we repay this national debt in the coin of the realm Sacagawea helped define."

Chronology

1790 Around this year, Sacajawea is born in the Lemhi River Valley, Idaho, as a member of the Shoshoni tribe.

1795 Around this year, Sacajawea is kidnapped by the Hidatsa Indians, who raise her as a member of their tribe and rename her Sacagawea, meaning "Bird Woman."

1803 President Thomas Jefferson obtains the Louisiana Purchase from France. He enlists Captains Meriwether Lewis and William Clark to explore the new territory and open a trail to the Pacific Ocean.

1804 The Corps of Discovery, headed by Lewis and Clark, leaves its camp outside St. Louis, Missouri, on May 14, and heads north up the Missouri River; on October 27 the expedition reaches the Five Villages of the Mandan Indians in North Dakota and makes camp for the winter. French Canadian fur trader Toussaint Charbonneau offers his services as an interpreter and cook. Charbonneau's wife, Sacagawea, also joins the expedition.

1805 Sacagawea gives birth to Jean Baptiste Charbonneau on February 11. The infant will become known as "Pomp" and be carried on his mother's back all the way to the Pacific Ocean; the Corps of Discovery, now accompanied by Sacagawea, leaves the Five Villages on April 7; the expedition camps on Shoshoni land in late July, marking Sacagawea's first return to her native land since she was kidnapped by the Hidatsa Indians as a young girl; on August 17, Sacagawea is reunited with her brother,

Cameahwait, who is now chief of the Shoshonis. Sacagawea serves as interpreter during an important council held with Lewis and Clark and Cameahwait in which the Shoshoni chief agrees to provide the Corps of Discovery with horses and guides; the Corps of Discovery makes camp for the winter at Fort Clatsop near the Oregon coast.

1806: Sacagawea guides a party led by Captain Clark through the Bozeman Pass and to the mouth of the Yellowstone River in July; the Corps of Discovery arrives back at the Five Villages of the Mandan Indians on August 17, and Sacagawea and Charbonneau leave the expedition; Lewis and Clark return to St. Louis on September 23, completing their expedition.

1812 On December 12, John Luttig, a fur trader and explorer, records the death of Sacagawea in his diary at Fort Manuel in South Dakota.

1884 An Indian woman about 94 years of age dies April 9 on the Wind River Shoshoni Reservation in Wyoming. Missionaries and Indians living on the reservation are convinced the woman was Sacagawea.

1999 The U.S. Mint unveils the new Sacagawea dollar coin in November.

Glossary

carcass–a dead body, especially that of an animal.

cloudburst–a sudden, heavy rainstorm.

Corps of Discovery–the name given to the expedition led by Lewis and Clark, whose purpose was to explore the newly acquired territory of the Louisiana Purchase and find a route to the Pacific coast.

council–a meeting of leaders or elders of an American Indian tribe.

expedition–a journey undertaken for a specific purpose such as exploration; a group of people who make such a journey together.

forage–to search for food.

interpreter–a person who can explain or translate, enabling two groups that do not share a common language to communicate.

keelboat–a riverboat with a very shallow hull that can be rowed, pulled, towed, or sailed.

marrow–a soft substance found in the cavities of bones.

missionary–a person who tries to convert people to his or her religion.

outpost–a frontier settlement.

papoose–an American Indian baby.

pirogue–a canoe-like boat.

plaque–a tablet that commemorates a person or event.

portage–to carry boats and supplies overland from one body of
water to another.

stockade–an enclosed area that can be easily defended, made by
planting wood posts side by side.

tepee–a movable, tentlike home used especially by the Plains
Indians that was made from animal skins draped over a
frame.

tiller–a long handle attached to a boat's rudder and used to steer
the boat.

tributary–a stream or river that feeds a larger river or body of
water such as a lake.

weirs–small, earthen dams used by some American Indian tribes
to trap fish.

Further Reading

Ambrose, Steven E. *Undaunted Courage: Meriwether Lewis, Thomas Jefferson and the Opening of the American West.* New York: Simon and Schuster, 1996.

Cavan, Seamus. *Lewis and Clark and the Route to the Pacific.* New York: Chelsea House Publishers, 1991.

Duncan, Dayton, and Ken Burns. *Lewis and Clark: The Journey of the Corps of Discovery.* New York: Alfred A. Knopf, 1997.

Holloway, David. *Lewis and Clark, and the Crossing of North America.* New York: Saturday Review Press, 1974.

Howard, Harold P. *Sacajawea.* Norman, Oklahoma: University of Oklahoma Press, 1971.

Kozar, Richard. *Meriwether Lewis and William Clark: Explorers of the Louisiana Purchase.* Philadelphia: Chelsea House, 2000.

Picture Credits

HAL MARCOVITZ is a reporter for the *Allentown (Pa.) Morning Call*. His work for Chelsea House includes biographies of explorers Marco Polo and Francisco Vazquez de Coronado, and the actor Robin Williams, as well as a history of terrorism in America and a history of the Apollo space program. He is the author of the satirical novel *Painting the White House*.